PRICELESS WORDS

Brittney,
You are such a delightful
person who knows you.
to those who know you.
Never lose your shine
in a world that so desperately
needs it. Best wishes!
Best wishes!
Lulu Rogers
2-20-21

PRICELESS WORDS

Poetry and Prose by

LISA PILGRIM

CONTENTS

Dedication   vi

1   LOVE   1

2   LUST   21

3   LONGING   42

4   LOSS   62

5   LIFE   82

6   LITTLE MORE   102

About The Author   122

To my priceless daughter, Monica.
Countless times over the past three years
you have patiently endured the question,
"Monica, Would you listen to this and
tell me what you think?"
This book would not be a reality
without your patience, and support.
I love you, and I appreciate you, Punkin Girl.

To Rick, my 289th Follower on Facebook.
If I had a nickel for every time
I've heard you say "You can do this."
I would be wealthy beyond imagination.
Though there are no nickels, I've grown rich
from your friendship, your advice,
and your unwavering support.
My humble thanks, kind Sir.

www.facebook.com/priclesswords1
pricelesswords1@gmail.com

Cover Design: Sarah Bowden of Star Blossom Art
            www.facebook.com/sarahbowden74
         https://www.numonday.com/shop/star-blossom-art/

First Printing: 2021

ISBN: 978-0-578-81144-4

CHAPTER 1

LOVE

Overthinker

Trust the overthinker who tells you they love you.
They have, most assuredly, thought of every reason not to.

Our Reality

Our connection is the strangest normal I have ever known.
Common sense says this makes no sense,
but my heart calls bullshit.
Each a mirror image of the other.
Yet, both of us failing to recognize the same value in ourselves.
My wish is that this dream truly is our reality.

Found

You found me,
and loved me,
when I found myself unlovable.

Touch Me

This moment has been years, and
tears, and fears in the making.
We stand face to face with all
walls down.
Just know that when you touch me
for the first time, you can't get any
closer than you've been before.
For you've already touched my soul.

Sunday Morning

I stand before your altar, my soul laid bare;
praying that I find words to give glory to your worth.

While at my darkest, your light shone down
until I was able to lift my head again.

While choking on betrayal, you breathed life
into my trust-weary soul.

While fearing attachment, I found my salvation
in your embrace.

For your unwavering devotion I owe a debt
that I will spend this lifetime repaying.

To you I surrender all that I have become, and
I vow to adore you until I draw last breath.

My Heart's Hero

You, single-handedly,
rebuilt the bridge between
despair and hope.
No matter the miles,
or the time between us,
you will forever be
my heart's hero.

From Heaven

Where did he come from?
This man who supports my every crazy idea,
celebrates every victory, and encourages me
through every defeat.

The same man who doesn't think me silly when I cry
over romantic memes, or when he sends me flowers
at work, for no reason.

The man that will stand toe-to-toe with me
when I get feisty and doesn't hesitate to tell me
I'm wrong, nor explain why he believes so.

This man who has stolen my heart must surely
have been dropped from Heaven.

Vengeance

I have something that I must tell you.
There's no need for you to reply, but
it's imperative that I get this off my
chest. I'm going to love you like
you've never been loved before.
Those others before me were
just playing around. I'm
going to love you with
a vengeance.

Tell The Story

I was thinking back to that first time, years ago, when you
invited me over. You lived in that tiny garage apartment.

Your favorite Harley blanket was spread out on the floor
and you had set up a picnic with really tall candlesticks
and candles that dripped colored wax.

You ordered pizza and the delivery guy almost died
laughing when he saw the spread. We laughed with him
just as hard. You poured beer into blue plastic champagne
glasses that you bought at the local discount store.

Frank Sinatra played in the background, and it was
magical. Then you handed me a small box wrapped
in purple paper because you knew it was my
favorite color.

Inside the box was a salt shaker shaped like an eggplant.
I knew that you chose the eggplant because it was purple,
too. I remember how puzzled I was by such a strange gift.

You held my face in both your hands telling me that it
was my one half year anniversary gift, and that I would
get the pepper shaker in six months.

As I stood there staring in your eyes, with tears streaming
down my face the CD changed to Barry White. It was so
romantic as we danced down the hallway.

The next morning I work up in the t-shirt that you went
to bed wearing.

Late

She takes her whiskey neat,
and her fun seriously.
She howls at the Crescent Moon
because the crowd is smaller.
Since forgiving herself
she forgives others more quickly.
And she's never late,
even though love is.

This One Is

You're concerned we have nothing new
to discover about love,
but there's no need to worry, my darling.
Yes, we've both done this before
and past failures seem to up the ante.
But, we have never been the two people
that we are right now, at this time in our lives.
Love may not be new to either of us;
but, this one is.

Fearlessly

I have loved fearlessly
with no waiver toward cowardice.
In shadow, and in total darkness.
Imagine how profoundly I will love
when love comes in light.

Innocence's Kiss

A bottle twist
Becomes a kiss,
On an Autumn's night years ago.

Innocent teens
As fate intervenes,
With the sudden garage light's glow.

Yet a smile remains
From memory's lane.
Of the kiss I'll never outgrow.

Intent

You love me quietly in gentle tones
that scream your heart's intent.

Holy Mess

She's a warm glass of whiskey.
Ice cold lemonade on a Summer's day.
She has no rhythm.
Loves dancing in the kitchen.
Wears hoodies with pearls.
Swears it's not sleeping nude
if you're wearing socks.
She's a special kind of chaos,
and he worships her holy mess.

A Tattered Heart

The edges are
rough and ragged,
on a barely beating heart
that's been taken for granted.

Most only notice
a stiff temperament,
not understanding it's a product
of its environment.

If consistently fed
with loyalty and lust,
till trust is established
and doubts are hushed.

Then lucky will be the soul
who wins the prize,
of all the love
a tattered heart can provide.

Chance

Given the chance, I intend to love you
in all the ways you believe love should.

Brand Me

At the hour of my death I pray I will have been
branded a fool for love. For have I not, then I will
not have loved fearlessly to the depths of my soul.

Missing - Part 1

I miss sex, but that's not what I miss the most.
I miss good morning kisses, goodnight kisses.
Someone I adore who thinks I'm pretty special, too.
A man's hand between my shoulder blades as we
cross the street.
I miss watching a man shave, or better yet,
helping him.
The way I fit under his arm as we snuggle while
watching TV.
That look he gives that tells me my heart is safe.
The feel of goosebumps as I lightly explore the
skin that covers his heart.
The sound of his breathing as he sleeps, contented,
beside me.
Waking in the morning to find my arm draped
over him, or vice-versa.
The way he challenges me to think, or to arm wrestling.
When I'm working on some task, and he comes up
behind me, pulls me close just to hold me for a moment.
Forehead kisses, neck kisses, warm slow kisses.
The 'I'm in a hurry, but this is much too important
to go without doing' kisses.
The tone of his voice when he whispers my name, or
talks about something he is passionate about, or
when he prays.
Grabbing on to his arm while walking, sliding my
hand down to his hand, which is open, and
waiting for mine.
Yes, I miss sex. But, not the kind of sex you can get
from just anyone.
No, I miss the kind of sex you get from The One.

Missing - Part 2

I miss lazy Sunday morning kisses that turn
into lazy Sunday morning love making.
Strong arms that won't let me fall on ice, and
a heart that didn't let me fall alone.
Looking into his eyes and knowing he sees
deeper than the color of my irises.
The feel of the skin on the inside of his
upper arm.
A giggle between the sheets.
Sharing a blanket, and popcorn, and soft
kisses, while watching a movie together
on a cold night.
Hearing him tell me that dinner was good
even though we both know it wasn't my
best, but he appreciates the amount of
love that went into it.
Meeting the gaze of a man who adores
me equally as much as I adore him.
Learning his favorite hobby, and while
I'll never be as proficient as he is, that's
not as important as the time we spend
together.
And sex. I miss sweaty, passionate,
soul deep, sex.

Point Of Entry

Entering someone's heart can be a tricky maneuver.
You must first locate a soft spot between all the scars.

Try Again

I dated a man off and on for seven years.
We were off and on because what we had
scared the hell out of both of us.

On our first date he said that he knew he
would never be able to stay away from me
because he knew he would never be able
to stay with me.

As silly as it sounds I knew with everything
inside me that I had never heard truer words.
When we weren't together we ached for
each other.
When we were, we were both terrified.
We learned to live only in those moments
that we were able to share.
We never knew how long one or the other
of us would be able to hold on.

The intensity of our connection showed no
signs of ease, even through all those years.
I no longer remember which one of us caved
first, but it was an amicable split.
That was the saving grace that allowed me
to survive it.

The memory of those moments when we
stood still, together, are eternally etched
into my soul.
I will carry them with me into the next
lifetime where we vowed to meet, and
try again.

Opportunities

You hold tightly to your
bruised heart. Attempting
to hide its scars as though
there is an ugliness in the
misfortunes of love. All
I see are opportunities to
show you love done right.

Daredevils

Love's for daredevils.
Grab your parachute baby;
We're about to fall!

Tragedy To Triumph

No reason nor rhyme
To this meeting in time,
Two souls thrown way off course.

Seemed company loved misery
As each shared their history,
Two lives overflow with remorse.

Better days had been seen
And while recollecting their dreams,
Two hearts began beating with force.

Like a stone breathed into life
Almost as if by design,
True love's random meeting the source.

Fuel

Goodbye fuels desire.
Wild fires rage.
No letting go.

Magnificent Light

Someone sharing the ups and downs of their life is
a gift given to the listener. How ever could we
claim to know someone without being aware of
their plight?
Yes, we are able to reinvent ourselves daily, but
those past pieces remain. They are what brought
us to this moment. Whether it be the best parts of
us, those points that we want displayed, or the worst
parts that we want no part of today...they all belong.
I thank you for trusting me with your shadows.
For without them I couldn't appreciate the
magnificence of your light.

Sigh

Have you ever heard the sound
a heart makes when it realizes
it's been found?
Experience has taught me that
it most resembles an Angel's sigh.

The Shirt Off Your Back

You keep your shirt sleeves
rolled up tightly.
Falsely believing you're
protecting the heart you
wear there.
By the time I get you out
of that shirt...
You'll give me both.

Something Together

He told of the emotions
that stirred his soul.
Of days when his sky
was dark, and nights
when the light wouldn't
allow sleep.

She spoke of the soul
that stilled her emotions.
Of days when the light
was blinding, and nights
when it was too dark to
allow sleep.

While they both knew they
couldn't be the other's
light, or dark; their desire
to be something together,
gave them both hope.

Epic Love

Timing and distance prove formidable foes,
For a blossoming love eager to grow.
Believing full well that their love will prevail,
For they recognize its epic scale.

Timing defeated by two patient hearts,
Distance conquered with the sharing of hearths.
Though their situation be not remedied soon,
He be forever her Wolf; She, eternally his Moon.

Equal Protection

A wounded heart beats inside the
chest of the Warrior who protects mine.

Through gallant effort he maintains
a personal oath to never inflict that
pain on another.

He proves his strength, and fortitude, by not
allowing his injuries to hold my innocent
heart responsible.

This heroism is the reason I will, steadfastly,
protect his damaged heart until I draw last breath.

Come Rest

Precious man,
Come take my hand,
You need a place to rest.

No one knows,
The hell you hold,
Inside your prideful chest.

You've been strong,
For far too long,
Please come and take a break.

Rest your soul,
And I will hold,
Your troubles 'til you wake.

When you rise,
'Fore we say goodbye,
Just know you're not alone.

Come fifty years,
I'll still be here,
My arms you can call home.

Quiet

Sometimes I am surprised at just how comfortable our quiet is.
With no demands to keep each other entertained the tranquility
provides
a peace filled sanctuary from the noises of the day.
I cherish these intervals when our only communication comes from
soft breathing, and two hearts beating in time.

Color Of Words

Eyes, dusty green with flecks of brown along the edges,
much akin to the changing oak leaves of an early fall,
and apt to turn as chalky blue as the skies of summer.

Lips, the same pink hue as the buttercups mixed with
the deep red clover that grows wild along a golden
sunlit red clay dirt road.

Arms of tan leather, baked by the Sun, that fold
perfectly around the milky white porcelain curves
of a woman.

How beautiful love is when painted
with the colors of words.

One Time

At one time I was certain that I would love you
for all my life, but now...
I know it won't end there.

Mr. Fix-It

Known as Mr. Fix-It, everyone brought him
their broken anythings, and he would put them
back together.
I handed over my heart, certain it would be his first failure...
I was wrong.

Hiding Place

I've spent years hiding
in plain sight.
Seen by many who
looked right through me.
Then you came along, and
suddenly I became visible again.
Now, my favorite hiding place
is in your arms.

Second Language

"If you could be fluent in any other language,
which would you choose?", he asked.

Without hesitation I replied,
"The language of Love.
It seems I can't speak it well enough to
carry on anything other than brief conversations."

"I will teach you.", he whispered.

My Calm

It's not the words you choose.
It's never the way you arrange them
into the sentences you deliver.
It is, as it has always been, the calm, confident,
certainty in the tone of your voice that
quiets the storm in my soul.

The Light Bringer

Wise beyond her years,
she knew that life would
serve up many dark days
for those that she loved.
So, she painstakingly
collected stars in a jar,
hell-bent on helping to
light their way.
Never did she realize that
for those who loved her...
she lit the stars.

Fighting For Love

We've been too many rounds to toss in the towel.
Let's leave the "you said/but then you said"
outside the ring and get back to the
bare knuckle basics of fighting on the same side.
Back to that time when our lips were the
only divider between our hearts, and
skin to skin was how our souls stayed connected.
Our love is worth fighting for.

Safe

This day took a lifetime to get here.
Two souls wandering crooked paths
that often ran parallel, but never crossed.
Disillusioned by love, yet not unbelieving that it exists.
Two hearts, safe, holding fast to the certainty
that the other isn't going anywhere.

CHAPTER 2

LUST

Fragrance

My favorite fragrance on a man
is when he's wearing just a hint
of last night's sin.

Taste

He tasted like
Whiskey & Whispers,
Smoke & Seduction,
Leather & Longing,
Wind & Wishes,
Mixed with Sweat &
just a hint of Sin.

The Ride

My imagination whisks me away to a memory
where tangled bodies create fire from sweat.
Primal songs echo for no one to hear,
except the angels,
as we disrupt Heaven's peace in gratifying release.

Otherworldly

In passion there is a difference between being passive,
and being submissive.
To be passive is to be indifferent, uninvolved,
in your own world.
To be submissive is to consciously participate
in something otherworldly.

Saving Grace

He thought her his saving grace.
Where her thighs met was where he worshiped.

The Perfect Storm

Angels scream as the demon
kisses the saint.
Pounding their fist on clouds
as their torrent of tears disgorge.
Their crackling chorus of despair
won't be silenced.
Yet, the lovers go undeterred.
Warm pools of ecstasy drench
the hell inside the angel while
flooding the demon's internal
heaven.
This, most unusual of unions,
creates the perfect storm.

Melt

You melted my heart...
all the way down to my panties.

Wild Child

There's a special kind of wild
In a Sunday's child,
No man has the strength to resist.

With a mischievous grin
On those lips made to sin,
As they cry out to be kissed.

But, beware of their tease
For your soul will bleed,
When you realize it was merely a tryst.

Love vs Lust

I have become skittish
in matters involving love.
Fortunately, not so in the
affairs of lust.

Art

A most priceless work of art is created
when two sweaty bodies meet satin sheets.

Lady Of Nightmares And Sin

The night casts shadows you thought you'd seen,
As a warm summer breeze stirs the sheets.

Two sensuous figures about to merge,
Relenting to lust's most primal urge.

You, a voyeur in slumberous trance,
Hypnotized by their erotic dance.

Resounding screams during passion's release,
As alone you satisfy your need.

You toss and turn awaiting night's end,
Knowing come sundown the liaison plays out again.

Who is this creature that haunts from within?
The mysterious lady of nightmares and sin.

Pedestal

I'm not the kind of girl who
likes to be put on a pedestal.
No, I'm the kind of girl who'd
rather be bent over one.

In The Night

Just as the Moon has two sides
so does love in the night.
The bright side   The dark side
where lovers   where blindfolds
lock eyes, and   cover hungry

eyes,

whisper sweet   howls and

moans

nothings, and   are the language,
make love on   and sex is shared
feather beds.   with wild aban-

don.

Smoldering Transgression

Desire ravaged by his flames.

My senses swirling as opaque
smoke penetrates my veins.

I want no forgiveness from
this lustful obsession.

He is my eternal
smoldering transgression.

Explorer

With the enthusiasm of an explorer
entering undiscovered territory,
you slid between my thighs.
Charting the landscape with dauntless
kisses you inched your way skillfully,
and hardily, towards the bounty.
A bold flick of the tongue successfully
opened rapture's floodgates, and I knew
I had been conquered long before you
had staked your claim.

Anticipation

Anticipation leaves us hell-bent on achieving ecstasy.
The lust in our bellies drown the butterflies
as our mouths fill from the overflow of orgasmic waves.
We fuck like we just remembered we can't swim.

Opportunity

The morning alarm beckons responsibility
as an overcast sky hides the Sun.
Habitude and honor guarantee compliance
while morning needs go unmet.
Armed with the belief that opportunity

sometimes comes disguised as gray days,
we crawl back under the blankets and
love away the dreary day.

Temptation

He whispered I love you
as though he were praying
for salvation. As though
not saying those words
would surely doom
him to hell.
Tonight, I intend to
lead him into temptation.

Angels Fall

She tried with all her
might to resist him.
Certain that even
salvation wouldn't
be able to wash
away his sin.
But, the heartbeat
between her thighs
controlled her as it
kept perfect rhythm
with his kisses.
Succumbing to desire,
and racked with guilt,
she forgets that the
mighty Lucifer himself
is proof that, undeniably,
even angels fall.

Bonfire's Dance

Red hot flames lick barren skin
until it, too, ignites.
Rising heat fans passion
as smoldering thighs unite.
It takes but a spark to flare up
an age old celestial dance.
I am his kindling, and he is
my bonfire on a moonless night.

Heat

It's just before dawn,
the night's interlude
still hangs on my lips.
For years I have held
you at arm's length
fearing that I would
land in the bed I made,
all by myself.
You relentless,
and I weak;
I succumbed.
With a voracious appetite
we feasted for hours
on raw lust.
I feel the Sun's fire
beginning to blaze
through the window.
I scoff at the heat
knowing it can't
hold a candle to ours.

ANTICIPATE

Arguably
Nothing
Teases like the
Interpretations of a
Conscious mind dwelling on the
Impending
Pleasure
Associated with
Titillating
Ecstasy.

Rain Dance

Wind and rain dance across the roof,
as I lie here alone. Sounds created are
akin to the soft, breathless, moans of
lovers writhing in passion's embrace.

Lightning so bright, that even with
eyes closed it causes muted flashes
through my eyelids. Reminding me
of my beloved's touch lighting up my
mind's eye, while I'm blindfolded.

Thunder startles, consistent with an
unanticipated touch across my bare
skin. Safe, yet breath stealing.

Oh, how I long for another
rain dance with you.

Naked Poetry

Meet me in my dreams where
we will make naked poetry.
As our tongues immerse in verse,
our limbs will intertwine in rhyme,
'til alas we achieve fruition
of our rhythmical composition.

Senseless

I love the smell of a fine cigar,
and leather.

The feel of satin,
and strong arms.

The taste of whiskey,
and wet kisses.

The sound of rain on a tin roof,
and a contented sigh.

The sight of a crackling fire,
and a man looking in my eyes
like he sees forever.

Intent

Don't kiss me with any less passion than the
intent of leaving your brand upon my soul.

Salty Poetry

Torsos tangle in rhythmic cadence
as voices blend in voracious verse.
An ages old composition scribbled in
various positions as sweat moistens
the sheets. A passionate rhyme repeats
through the night, and I wake to salty
poetry on my lips.

Care To Join Me

Animalistic
Attraction?
Boudoir
Beguilement?
Cocktails &
Carousing?
Delicious
Destination?
Energizing
Entanglement?
Frolicking
Fun?
Care to join me?

Muscle Car

Young hearts yearned, and innocence turned
in the back seat of that muscle car.

By Design

Passion filled promises
laced with lust,
For two sensual souls
bound by trust.

Surrendering their hearts,
their bodies do follow.
Cherishing their time
as if it were borrowed.

In sweat they writhe,
bodies entwined.
Pure passion and lust,
by the Universe's design.

Bliss

Love is not a sedated state of lust.
Love is lust set in motion.
When the two are in unison,
Bliss is formed.

Living Poetry

You were my first piece of living poetry.
Spewing words of lust and love while
my tongue was tangled in your rhyme.
I endlessly searched for the synonym
for forever, or eternally.
Words that didn't come, but oh how I did.

Naughty Butterflies

Modern day romance
seems hard to summarize,
As texting and video chats
become commonplace in our lives.
Still our connection
can't be denied,
When just the sight of your face
gives me naughty butterflies.

The Moon And The Tide

You the Moon, and I the tide
longing for your fullness to pull me in.
Rising and falling to the rhythm of your will
as your hands guide my hips.
Lips to lips as the waves break the shore.
Desperately, and repeatedly flooding
our bodies, and our souls
before daybreak separates us once again.

Testify

My fall from grace began after being baptized
in a puddle between firm thighs.
The threat of damnation wields no power,
and I've no want for redemption
now that I have visited Heaven.

Real Cravings

She has a veracious appetite for
which she offers no apologies.
Exacting in expectations, she
has left many a good man with
shortness of breath and bulging slacks.
Opportunities are abundant, yet
insecurity is fed by doubts that
love and lust can be synonymous.
She craves both.

Dance With Me

Come dance with me
on satin sheets.
We'll share a waltz
of passion's release.
A perpetual rhythm
with no regard of time.
Sharing a dance
that lasts a lifetime.
Take the lead
and I will follow.
'Til our voices blend
in sweet vibrato.

Us

Ravenous lust
Spontaneously combust.
Describes us.

Fireworks

Great sex isn't always parades
with marching bands and fireworks.
Often, at its best, it's simply an
intimate sharing of vulnerabilities.

Bruise

I intend to kiss you so deeply,
that I leave a dark purple bruise
on your heart.

Holy Water

You are the whisper
in my prayers.
The words
in the hymn my soul sings.
And, the holy
in the water between my thighs.

Again

Face to face,
We kept pace,
Till we quaked.
We ached to do it again.

RESEARCH

Reciprocal
Endeavors in
Sexual
Experimentation,
Agreed upon by adults, often
Results in
Concurrent,
Harmonious, ecstasy.

Life Quiz

Life Quiz:
Define Mind-Blowing Sex.

Young, Foolish Me:
It's the orgasm you achieve when
your bodies are in sync.

Older, Wiser Me:
It's the ecstasy you achieve when
your souls are in sync.

Sealed

Bodies tangle in moist sheets,
Glowing in the aftermath of passion's breach.
I gaze into your eyes and I know that our
eternity is sealed at this moment.

CLANDESTINE

Couples
Linger
Among
Night time shadows
Determinedly
Enjoying
Surreptitious
Trysts
In hopes of experiencing
Neglected
Ecstasy.

Baptized

I can no longer tell the difference between
Hellfire and Holy Water.
All along I knew you were the devil incarnate.
Yet, I wanted nothing more than to be
baptized in your sin.

DELICIOUS

Delectable
Endeavors,
Lascivious
Interactions,
Carnal
Incidents,
Offer us
Ubiquitous
Satisfaction.

Determined

Visions of the Sun's glow on tangled torsos
creates heat between cold sheets generating
that old familiar yearning.
I love to see the sunrise through the eyes of
the one who is equally adoring of me.
I fantasize about the morn I wake to you beside
me determined to satiate my need.

Drowning

Surfing atop soaked sheets,
Waves of desire drench us.
Drowning in carnal bliss,
I've no want for salvation.

Ardor

Little did anyone know
we were two friends
waging naked war
with unrelenting ardor.

Primal Peace

Required conformity comes at a steep price
as daily routines force obligations on a soul
that knows neither quit, nor quiet. As the day
fades away, cinched tightly in the freedom of a
leather corset, safe in the hands of the man
who feels her pain, she finds her primal peace.

Make Plans

Let's cut through the pretense;
I know you feel the same heat
that I feel.
There's no need to pussy foot
around the subject.
It's time to make a plan to meet
and sheet.
Just so we're clear...I want
nothing to do with your heart.

Memoir

Our memoir would make Angels blush.

Who But Me?

Who but me knows where your demons hide?
Who but me can coerce them out to play?
Who but me lit that flame you'd long denied?

Tonight you'll crawl into that cold, vanilla bed,
fulfill her needs, and she'll roll over to peaceful
slumber.
But, you will toss and turn, and want for more.
Because who but me can fulfill yours?

CHAPTER 3

LONGING

Recognition

Caution:
Words read here may cause goosebumps.
Words of truth,
that your soul recognizes,
often do.

Reality

The cool breeze raises goosebumps
along your ribs begging my tongue
to connect the dots.
Knowing this will raise more than
the hairs on your chest, I straddle
your hips in anticipation.
My lips find their way through the
valley of your collarbone, across the
ridge of your jawline, and to the
soft hills of your lips.
As the sun breaks through the
window I will rise, and keep living
for the day when this dream
becomes a reality.

Perfection

Intoxicating longing whispers
in a kiss done right.

Forgiven

I write my wrongs,
knowing full well
that this ink will
never offer absolution.
Merely hopeful that
through reflection
I will be able to
forgive myself.

Illusion

There is a yearning deep
inside my soul. A desire
that I don't recognize, yet
somehow it seems strangely
familiar. As surely as I am
all that I am, I stand
knowing that all I see is
not all there is to me.

That's All

All I ever wanted
was to be all you ever wanted.

Yearning For Home

The pit of your arm,
a comfort by design.
Nestling children,
with love you oblige.

Clutching the scared,
safe and snug.
Supporting friends
in a soothing hug.

A simple bend of the arm
seems of little concern,
Yet my soul screams it's the home
for which it yearns.

Grandma's House

Picking daffodils and hyacinths
but not the roses with their thorns.
Drinking straight from the hose
when parched from hours of hide-and-seek
behind the hydrangeas, and the crepe
myrtle bushes.
Picking blackberries from the huge
bush out by the back gate that led to
the chicken house.
That chicken house smelled awful
and had flies, but gave us the eggs
that became the best breakfasts and
baked goods that anyone had ever tasted.
Planting rocks as headstones in the
Pet Cemetery where every creature was
buried. From Joe, the trusty German Shepherd,
to a garden snake whose head was chopped
off by a sharp shovel when Grandma
overheard our screams.
What I wouldn't give to spend another
Summer outdoors at Grandma's house.

The Breeze

Up above the trees
The breeze stirs old memories.
Bound to forever.

Soon

The setting Sun casts shades
of deep orange and yellow,
on the cream colored linens
of the bed.
The nest where we whisper
promises, laugh like children,
and make love with a passion
so intense that for a brief
moment our souls merge.
Sitting on the edge of the
bed, basking in the last
moments of the Sun's
warmth; counting down
the minutes until you are
home to satisfy the heat
building inside of me.

I Remember

I lick my lips, and whisper your name.
Remembering the way you tasted as you rolled off my tongue.

Drug Of Choice

How will I put Us behind me
when I crave you all the way to
my core?
When your lips are the harm
that my soul cries out for?
How damn stupid can one be
when Love is their drug of choice.

Manifestation

I sit in silence as my mind speaks.
It tells tales of hope, strength, and
ensuing abundance.
As surely as belief sprouts from
my soul, I will manifest an opulent
future into reality.

Temporary Bliss

Years ago a Seer
declared that I
would know bliss.
I simply wish
she had divulged
that it would only be
temporary.

Fall

Fall is the constant reminder
of how much I want to be
wrapped up in one of your
old flannel shirts...
while it's wrapped around you.

Private Eyes

There was a time when she could turn a man's head.
Raven hair with a sparkle in her eyes, and a smile that
guaranteed his lips would upturn. Round, tan-skinned,
breasts that pointed the way to a man's heart. Curved
hips that begged to be pulled in closer, and tight thighs
that hypnotized the hardest of men. Yet, she was never
quite comfortable in her own skin.

Now the years have flown, her raven hair is sprinkled
with silver. Though her skin's not as taut, her eyes still
light up as she flashes a smile at him. Rounder hips,
softer thighs, her breasts sit a little lower on a her chest,
but her nipples still lead the way. Her confidence?
Her confidence soars because of his love. And, she
gladly bares her body for his private eyes.

Seek More

I seek more than someone
who can crawl between my thighs,
and make me scream.
I'm searching for the one
who can also climb inside my anguished heart,
and make those screams go silent.

The Whole

I am terrified of falling
into the whole of wanting you,
and not finding you there.

Include Me

You don't realize that every beat
of your heart scatters new stars
throughout the Universe.
Or, that I wish upon every one
for your happiness...all the while
hoping that happiness includes me.

Choices

You can keep your cordial dinners,
and Saturday night lovemaking.
I'm looking for a strong shot of whiskey,
and a fuck in the rain.

Smiling Eyes

Pursed lips offer no tell-tale
sign of recognition between
two souls meeting for the
first time, in a lifetime.

Arms outstretch for a
friendly greeting as
they lock in a gaze of
smiling eyes.

Each recognizing a soul
they've known before
and silently offering
thanks to the Universe
for a chance to get
it right this time.

Help Wanted

Seeking a proofreader
for all the unwritten poems
still inside my soul.

Balance

I'm searching for the one who understands,
and appreciates, the importance of both the
masculine and feminine roles in a relationship.

A soul who guards and honors their role as
the world recognizes it, yet knows that within
the sanctity of the relationship the roles can,
and should, switch if the need arises.

Honoring both the masculine and feminine
strengths that reside within us makes for a
happier, healthier, more balanced union.

I Wait

Balancing on the horizon
of wants and wishes
as timing tips the scales.
Desire has no expiration date.
So, I wait.

The One

You rise with the Moon,
a wolf on the prowl.
Hunting for a mate who's
unafraid of your growl.

Tired of the plight,
you're growing weary.
Belief in love as
your determination
becomes bleary.

Hold out sweet Prince
until the light of the Sun.
And you just might find,
I am the one.

The End

You whisper my name like it's a mystery.
Softly, quizzically, as if you're trying to solve
the riddle of how I stole your heart.
Just remember, the guilty never kiss and tell,
and secrets are never revealed until the end.

World's Weight

Your memory weighs on my heart with the
gravity of every "what if" my mind can imagine.

Indelible Ink

You've worked your way under my skin.
You've changed the colors of my life
from shades of gray to cheerful yellows,
serene blues, and passionate reds.
Please, please, tell me that you have used indelible ink.

Utter Silence

I've voiced countless words
through the tip of a pen,
but I fail to force my lips to utter the words
my soul longs to scream.

Rough Seas

I've never been demanding of love.
Always allowing it to ebb and flow like the tide.
Relishing the highs, and centering during the lows.

Yet, just as the red sky that morn foretold,
I met up with your rough seas.
You have tossed about my calm conviction on love,
and now I'm unsure the course.

Sitting anchored on a calm sea would be far safer,
but the raging storm that is your love, is my weakness.

Tender Tears

Please don't be alarmed if you notice
a tear rolling down my cheek.
I call them Tender Tears.
They spill over because you have touched
a place in my heart that hasn't been touched
in a very long time.
One typically associates tears with loss,
but those tender tears are bringing
my heart back to life.

Visions

I reach to touch
your curled hand
and you flinch.
Even in your
deepest slumber
you withdraw
from my
wanting touch.
You, unknowingly,
instigate a painful
twinge deep inside
my chest as my
eyes attempt to
wash away visions
of a time when
we were in love.

Not Deterred

As the days grow shorter
I long to spend nights
curled up in the warmth
of your embrace.
Distance and circumstance
sabotage the experience that
my soul imagines to be bliss.
Yet my heart isn't dissuaded.

Shame

Life is full of fucking shames.

Wake Me

Wake me and take me
out of these dreams.
To a place far away
where love is all it should be.
Where lips are for kissing,
not degrading screams.
And, the arms that hold you
never take swings.
I'm counting on you
to be all that you seem.
Who ever you are...
wherever you are...
Please wake me and take me
out of these dreams.

Peace

I am at peace
with my solitude,
but have a deep
need to share it
with someone else.

Screams

Morning rituals leave little time
for the mind to wander. The
daylight offers but a brief respite
from the repeating nightmare.

As night falls, monsters escort
in the loneliness. Moonlight
filtering in through drawn
curtains casts an eerie shadow
of the one who isn't here.

The horror is heightened when
crawling into a cold bed to find
no arms to hold you. Yes, it is
in the stillness of a long night that
the yearning screams the loudest.

Disguise

Desire can disguise
a dream, or a demon.
Loneliness makes it
impossible to tell
which is which.

Dance With Me

Dance with me through my mind
and you will find that you are
mingled into every thought.

Dance with me through my dreams
and you will discover that you are
intertwined with every wish, every hope,
and every vision I have of the future.

Dance with me inside my heart and you
will know that you are the only partner there.

Lead Me Home

Two lost souls,
not without hope,
hungrily searching
for proof that forever
love does exist.
Maybe it's an outdated
notion, maybe it's a
fool's dream. Or just
maybe, the fates will
conspire to reward
their perseverance,
and finally lead their
hearts home.

Rain Dance

As I lie here alone, wind causes
the rain to dance across the roof.
Creating sounds akin to the soft,
breathless, moans of two lovers
writhing in passion's embrace.
The lightning so bright that even
with eyes closed it causes muted
flashes through my eyelids. A
gentle reminder of my beloved's
warm touch. The same touch
that lit up my mind's eye while
blindfolded.

The churning storm outside
makes me yearn for another
rain dance with you.

Truth

Lessons learned about love from liars,
leave the lonely longing for truth.

Love Back

I long for a relationship so safe
that I no longer associate being
vulnerable with becoming a victim.
Arms that provide such a sense of
security that I can at last lay down my
shield and be tender without fear.
And, a heart that makes me feel so
cherished that I love back with a vengeance.

Wait

I was born of falling stars,
and though I landed first
I will wait for you. For my
soul craves continuance
with yours.
This lifetime offers us
another chance at love's dance,
and I will wait for you.

Two Hearts

Flickering flames cause light to dance on the bare skin of entwined
lovers.
Beads of sweat that glisten in the candle's glow become the streams
that flow across the dermal coverings of two hearts.
Two hearts afraid of the heat, yet both knowing they're going to risk
the burn.

Only Then

Tonight is one of those endless nights.
I can't unwind, can't relax.
I'm exhausted and in desperate need of calm.
But, my soul is stirring with a relentless,
ages old, longing that won't let me go.
If only my heart were able to convince it
that you will indeed return to us...
there would be peace in my soul.

Ghost

I'm that cool wisp of air
across your chest
as you undress.
I'm that scratch down
your back as you climb
into bed.
I'm that whisper of a
moan that you hear as
you lay down your head.
And, I'm that ache
between your thighs
that does not let you rest.

Hurry

The rhythm of the Moon stirs in my soul
as distant howling reminds me how best it be satiated.
There's little time before the morning light.
Won't you please, please, hurry?

Circumstance

Circumstance leaves us tongue tied,
and tight lipped.
Both knowing the truth in words
we dare not utter.
Yet, neither allowing timing
to deter the tie.
Rituals enforce the bond
that chance connected.
The same bond that circumstance
can not break.

Last Wish

My final wish will be that
I draw my last breath while
your lips are pressed to mine.
My prayer is that the kiss will hold
me until you join me for eternity.

No Chance

Time stands no chance of erasing your memory
when every other thought in my head
puts you back in my bed.

Bring On The Night

Day holds its demons,
thieves of precious time,
when longing is the language
between your heart and mine.
So, we'll rage against the light,
and pray it quickly fades,
so that we may return
to the world that love made.

Woven

I yearn to be so close that I am able
to weave in and out of you.
To wrap my arms around you so tightly
that we are able to merge.
I ache to touch you where you've never been touched.
I long to feel your Soul.

CHAPTER 4

LOSS

Poetry

Poetry is simply a collection of dried tears.
Dried tears of joy, of hope, of longing, of loss, of love,
and of every possible emotion.
Poetry is dried tears arranged in a manner
so that it is understood by the reader
whose tears are still wet.

Nothing

From across a linen pillow
I have stared into eyes sparked
by flames of desire.
Felt the ferocious hunger in
frothing lips as they pressed
so hard against mine that I felt
certain we would meld together.
Received the marks of raw passion
as you tugged hungrily at my curves.
Heard the guttural tones of your
primal growl as your hips thrust
your undulating manhood deep
into my soul.
Listened to your vows of eternity
while cradled in your arms after
love's release.
So, please forgive me when I
find it impossible to believe it
all meant nothing.

Accident

The sun fades early on a Winter's eve,
While darkness offers no reprieve.
As a wary heart struggles to believe,
What my mind can't conceive.
Happily Ever After was deceived,
Though to that dream I'll forever cleave.
Left by love and left to grieve,
The choice not yours to up and leave.

Dawn Breaks

Up all night when the sun breaks the horizon.
Lamenting over choices that didn't allow
me a choice.
Wonder if losing you would have hurt less
had you died.
The only certainty is that it would have, had I.

We Just Disagree

We agreed to disagree,
and it wasn't long
before we didn't speak at all.

Waiting Down The Road

Past the Pearly Gates and I'd like to know,
Which way is it to the fishing hole?
Yes, Heaven's streets are paved with gold,
But, where do all the country folk go?
While the mansions are a beautiful site,
I'll have to pass, if that's all right?
You see I'm looking for the country
and the humble abodes,
Because I'm sure my Daddy,
will be waiting down the road.

Be Brave

"Be Brave" they tell a 16 year old girl as the
steel gray coffin hovers over a black abyss.
The final resting place of the skin and bones
that are left from the home that housed the
immortal soul of the man who was her father.

"Be Brave" they say as she stands on knees
that refuse to lock, and she crumbles.
The bright red clay from a freshly dug hole
smears on her new black skirt. The stain
to be carried home like a souvenir from an
event, that she had a front row seat to, that
fate forced her to attend.

"Be Brave" she hears from inside her heart over
the screams from lungs that make no sound.
She recognized the voice and makes a resolution
to withstand any pain that this cruel world
throws at her, knowing she will be brave because
he is still with her, inside her heart.

Lessons

The bridge I couldn't bring myself to burn.
Taught me a lesson I'll never unlearn.
Love can be deceitful though it may seem pure.
And, Angels lose their wings when they're unsure.

Best - A Ten Word Story

You are the best thing that I ever fucked up.

Colorful Disaster

There is an artful beauty in sorrow.
The depth of the pain adds a thick,
ebony shadow to the physical features
of the wounded.
Incessant pounding creates aubergine
and umber bruises on a barely
beating heart.
The rawness of the pain paints murky,
crimson clouds in the mind.
All while the soul is enveloped
in a dismal indigo cloak.
Each adornment of this wretched,
beautiful, disaster creates poetry.

Can't Forget - A Six Word Story

A good memory is merciless punishment.

Damn Shame

You're pulling against us,
and it's pulling us apart.
The tighter I hold on,
the tighter the hold on my heart.
When love becomes a childish game
everyone loses.
Damn, what a shame.

Afterlife

I want to meet up with you
in the afterlife, and review
the time we shared.

Reminisce about all the hours
spent sharing dreams, and
schemes, and childhood things.

Recollect the secrets,
fears, and tears shared
throughout our years.
And, as we reflect back
on all the love, I would
ask the question that I
never braved before...
Why did you let me go?

Distance - A Six Word Story

Distance grows as silence gets louder.

Battle Scars

She'll listen to your battle stories,
offering valuable advice from the
years of experience she has gained
while fighting her own wars.
Yet, so as never to appear weak,
or possibly to protect her sanity,
she'll never speak of the one she lost.

Acceptance

Limping down to the river's edge,
maneuvering through the sharp, slippery
rocks of my memories. I sit sifting through
the ashes of the bridge you burned
searching for understanding. Dusting the
soot from the hands that long to touch you;
I realize this darkness won't soon wash off.

The fire that was Us burned white hot
on promises, and good intentions. It's
going to take years, and tears, to clean
the sediment that now stains my heart
without answers to scrub it.

But you never know, if I have enough
faith, and I don't give up, maybe somewhere
in this devastation I will find acceptance.

Roll The Dice

When rolling love's dice circumstance is the enemy,
and timing may well be its executioner.

Green

In the most spiteful of tones you told me to
go find someone who was "worthy" of me.
That's exactly what I did.
As fate would have it our paths have crossed
again tonight.
Might I say, that shade of green
your wearing is very unbecoming.

The Boy With The Crooked Smile

Your bald head resting on the crisp white pillowcase; your eyes closed in peaceful slumber. I run my thumb, lightly, across your wrinkled brow as my thoughts wander through the past 40 years.

In my mind's eye I see that sandy brown haired boy with the crooked smile, standing on the ramp at the football field on that brisk October night. Leaning on the rail, so calm, so cool, waiting for me. He flashed that million dollar smile, and I melted.

The confident teenager in a military uniform determined to make a good life your new wife.

The proud young father of two. First, a son with dark hair like his mother. Then, a daughter with your same crooked smile.

The broad shouldered man who helped carry his father to his final resting place.

The middle aged man with grown children with children of his own. Hundreds of hours spent of a bike, relaxing, regrouping, and rediscovering life as time now finally allows.

The balding man recalling childhood stories with a tear rolling down his cheek as his mother slips away.

Forty years filled with extremes in finances, relationships, and health. Yet, I still see that sandy brown haired boy with the crooked smile who took a chance when he spoke to that shy girl that brisk October night. (Continued)

A tear escapes my eye as I kiss your wrinkled brow.
As the lid closes I begin to sob uncontrollably, remembering
that night, 40 years ago, when a shy girl didn't have the nerve to
speak back to that sandy brown haired boy with the crooked smile.

Wanderer's Heart

Vagabond bones shelter a wanderer's heart.
No time for roots as you'll soon depart.
Although you've meant no other heart harm,
Nary a one was able to hold your charm.
But I've no doubt I'll eternally be part,
Of your vagabond bones, and your wanderer's heart.

Visions

I reach to touch your curled hand
and you flinch.
Even in the deepest of slumber you
withdraw from my wanting touch.
You unknowingly instigate a painful
twinge deep inside my chest as my
eyes attempt to wash away visions of
a time when we were in love.

Unspent Dreams

Bury me with our unspent dreams
so that I may have something to hold on to
while I wait for you.

That Song

I met up with an old friend today,
Believing the feelings were locked away.
Our time together was but a brief visit,
Not lasting more than a few short minutes.
All the memories I'd believed safely stored,
Came flooding out with each tear I poured.
Immense feelings I'd thought long gone,
Escaped my heart when I heard that song.

Hollowness

Time torments with every heartbeat
beyond the hollowness of losing you.

Frozen

Shivering as the ice cold breeze brushes
the back of my bare neck where warm
lips once met skin. Frigid air burning
my lungs as I struggle to remember
the warmth of his bare chest pressed
against my naked breasts. Kneeling on
frozen ground before the slab of granite
that bears the only remembrance of
the details of the life of the man whose
passion burned white hot. Mourning
the man who now slumbers beside
strangers rather than in my arms, as I
struggle to keep my shivering heart
from freezing.

Final Climb

Let's climb onto this bed and forget
that it will be the last time.

In remembrance of our journey, let
me feel the warmth of your lips as
they nibble and tug at the skin that
covers my heart. Let me map your
body with my fingernails, scaling
down the soft underside of your arm,
along your rib cage, across your hip,
curving around to the inside of your
thighs as I make my way to the apex
where our bodies meet.

As we ascend to the heavens I'll
scream your name in ecstasy without
considering that the next time it rolls
across my lips it will be in agony.

Please leave while I sleep so that
when I crawl from this bed in the
morning you won't see me fall.

Suspension

I am suspended in time.
Inhaling oxygen that my
lungs refuse to release.
Caught between what
was our last kiss,
and the goodbye
that was never uttered.

Only Ever

It is impossible to think of you
in the past tense when I only
ever saw you as my future.

My Immortal

The world will know of your hazel eyes with tiny brown flecks,
and how those eyes turned dark green juxtaposed with your red
cheeks when you got angry.

How you always lit a cigarette before cranking your bike, and
even years after you quit smoking you would instinctively
reach into your shirt pocket after you had climbed on.

That you enjoyed sparring with words. But secretly didn't
mind losing as you wanted others to feel they had gotten one up
on you.

Or, that the dish you missed most after your mother had
passed was her Chicken & Dumplings.

Saying "I'm sorry" was hard for you, but "I love you" came easily.

When you kissed me, you wrapped your left arm around my
ribs, and planted your hand on the small of my back.
Placing your right hand on my cheek with your thumb resting
just below my eye, pinky tucked under my jaw while your
other three fingers wrapped up in my hair. Then you would
pause, and stare in my eyes before you pulled me in for a kiss.

You are immortal because you were loved by a writer.

Memories

Still waters run deep as my memories,
and the proof comes with every sunrise.
Each new day an opportunity to remember,
review, and retell the stories that made up
our life together, and I am blessed beyond
measure. When the time comes to face my
final sunset, I will be giddy with anticipation
knowing that my next sunrise will be with
you by my side once more.

See Me

See me. I'm the girl with the
sad eyes, and cowered stance.
The one beaten down by
inglorious lovers.

Aimlessly, being led by an
ancient soul bound to the
notion that true love exists.

Nursing my heart's bruises
as my soul whispers of grand
illusions, like trust, and hope,
and happiness.

My desperate plea is that she
come to understand what my
heart has accepted; in this
lifetime, there are only lessons.

Faded Canvas

Layers of paint cover the faded
canvas that is my life.
Each time I am forced to start
over, the bruises change the color
of my soul, leaving their darkness.
I fear that with many more strokes
I will completely vanish into the black.

Feathers

Feathers fall where Angels tread,
Proof of existence they lovingly shed.
A right they earned that goes unsaid,
So those they love be not mislead.
Though you'll not see them,
They are not dead.

Unspoken

I sit here with a stranger in a dark, dank room,
Wondering how we ended up inside this tomb.
It seems there's a me who's long lost and forgotten,
And, a heart upon which hard times have fallen.
Who knew we'd end up so lonely and broken,
Simply because our pride left three words unspoken?

Loved And Lost

To have loved, wholly, and lost
is to die without ever crossing
the threshold between this world,
and the afterlife.

You Tried

You'll think me foolish
and I can accept that.
But, dammit, I loved you.
I loved you, and I choose
to remember that you
tried to love me, too.

Blame

My mind is drained by dreams
that never came to fruition.
My will is exhausted
to the point of submission.
My soul questions
how we got into this condition.
While my heart simply answers,
"Blame it all on love's attrition."

This Is A Recording

We're sorry, but you have reached a love
that has become disconnected, and is no
longer observed.
If you feel you have reached this love in
error, please hang up and dial either
party, individually, again.

Dead Flowers

Flowers once red as a lover's lips,
Delivered by hands with a passionate grip.
Love was made 'neath those blooms so bright,
Never expecting it be our last time.
A dozen roses well past their prime,
Much like the love of your heart for mine.

Leave The Door Open

I recognize the cawing of the crows in the distance
as they wait to feed on what's left of the
shattered heart you're leaving behind.
Weakened by each broken promise, each lie,
each deception; too beat down by love's plight
to possibly fend them off.
They've slowly pecked away, devouring my heart
little by little.
As you go, please leave the door open so they
can make this fast.

Priority

This isn't the first time my
heart and I have parted ways.
You see, lifetime after lifetime,
she always chooses you as her
priority.
Maybe in the next lifetime
you'll return her to me.

Stages

Now that you're gone
my greatest aspiration
is to reach the
comfortably numb stage.

Fading Memories

In the middle of an ordinary day...
a memory strikes.
Tears flood, attempting to extinguish the fire in my chest.
The source of which is this burning desire for you
that still smolders inside my rib cage.
I choke back the pain knowing
that while this may well kill me,
death will be imminent
once the memories have all faded away.

Spill

When I think of you
the memories spill onto my cheeks.

3 AM

It's 3 AM and the only sound
is the heartbeat pounding
in my temple splashing
around in the pool of tears
on my pillow.

How?

It seems there are no rules for unraveling two lives,
but before we become strangers again may I ask a
couple of questions? I would like to be somewhat
prepared in the event that I am ever able to try and
fall in love again.

Will he know when he kisses me to put his hand
behind my head which causes me to instinctively
tilt my head back to rest in his palm without nary
a thought of such on my part? Will he recognize
that this makes it very easy for him to kiss, and
nibble on my neck? Will he know this will make
me weak in the knees?

Will he have learned that just before we kiss,
when our lips are ever so close, he is to draw in a
deep breath which takes mine away? Will he know
this gives the sensation of being pulled inside him?
And, makes the kiss so much deeper?

Are these things that all men know? If not,
then how will I ever fall in love again?

Picture Frame

In a dusty picture frame on a night stand by a bed.
There's a black and white photograph of a love
she shan't forget.
In Soldier's dress she held him close
unknown of where he would roam.
Today's the day she'll again see her son
for today's the day God called her Home.

Be Here Now

You always fell asleep with your head on my chest.
I would tease you, and say that you just wanted
your face between my boobs. We would have a
laugh before falling asleep.
Last night, after all these years, you changed our
routine. When it came time for your reply you
raised up, looked me in the eyes, and said very
seriously, "That's not it. That's really never been
it. I just love hearing your heartbeat whisper
my name." We didn't laugh. We made love.
For the last time.
Oh God, why can't you be here now?
Without you to whisper to, I fear my heart
will have no reason to beat.

Memory Lane

Today I took a walk down our Memory Lane.
I visited places I never thought I'd see again.
Just an old dirt road with potholes.
As I maneuvered our obstacles I began to see
the price that each had cost.
I froze short of the fork where we got lost.

Heat

The heat you radiated melted my resolve.
Your smoldering passion left my mouth
parched, and my soul searing.
Yet, the ice in your veins offered no relief
to the charred heart you left behind.

CHAPTER 5

LIFE

Masterpiece

I don't want to fix you,
and I can't heal you.
But, maybe I can help you to see
just how beautiful your broken is.
Each cracked piece fits
into the masterpiece of
who you are right now.
And, right now, I see a beautiful soul.

Cling

Though life may breed doubt
I cling to the notion
that tenderness exists.

Everyone's A Poet

You write poetry every time you:
Cuddle a newborn baby,
Laugh a belly laugh with your best friend,
Belt out your favorite song along with the radio,
Look through an old family photo album,
End a relationship, whether good or bad,
Hold the hand of someone as they draw last breath,
Stand up for an underdog,
Say "I love you", or say "I'm sorry".
You see, poetry is simply summing up
those increments of life in words.

Ripples

Ripples of unknown origin
tickle the shore as a reminder
that there is beauty to be found
even when our calm quivers.

Time

People who are barely hanging on
are often the ones who take the time
to keep others from letting go.

Power Of Words

Never underestimate
the power of a sincere
"I was an asshole, and
I'm sorry."

Transformation

Yes, of course I've changed...
How else could I become
who I'm supposed to be?

Exercise

Jump to someone's rescue.
Lift someone's spirits.
Run from gossip
Throw caution to the wind.
Bend your head in thanks.

Manifest

Clear vision and unrelenting perseverance are the tools
for manifesting your heart's desires.

Dream Today

Today I'm dreaming with my eyes wide open.
And while I can't see the future...
I can feel hope.

My Tribe

I've always been drawn to
broken souls. Funny, I
never realized it's because
I belong to their tribe.

It's What Matters That Counts

Don't count the tears you've cried,
there are far too many. Possibly,
just as many as all the mistakes
you've made. And, most likely,
as many as the regrets you've
racked up.
Instead, count the number
of times you've managed
a smile when all you wanted
to do was cry.
Count each time you've had
the courage to right a wrong.
And, don't forget to count
every single time that you've
been able to forgive yourself.
These times are the true measure
of your worth.

Burden

"Burden" doesn't exist
where love lives.

Change

Butterflies and tears
are God's way of
reminding us that
although it is often
a painful struggle
there is beauty in change.

Out Loud

This life has been a long, hard, read.
While a rewrite is not a possibility,
a new chapter is beginning.
A plot change is the perfect time to lock the shift key, and
LIVE LIFE OUT LOUD!

My Makeup

I'm made mostly of wishes,
and memories,
and dreams that almost came true.

Fertilizer

Life serves up plenty of shit.
The choice you must make
is to get bogged down by it,
or to spread it around like fertilizer,
and grow!

Taste

Passion and Poison
often leave the same
aftertaste.

These Hands

You look and all you see are old, wrinkled hands,
but I see hands that have wiped spills and noses,
butts and tears.
Hands that have patted the backs of countless hurting friends.
Hands that have done hard work and cooked many a meal.
Hands that held that one true Love of a Lifetime.

As you look at these old, wrinkled hands, let me fold them
in prayer for you as I have done every day of your life.
Let me utter one last request,
to The One who designed these hands,
that you too, will live long enough,
and have loved deeply enough,
so that at the end of your days
your hands may look just like mine.

Soul Food

Find the one
who feeds your soul
instead of your ego,
and you'll never go hungry again.

Whatever

When sarcasm and apathy collide,
every "Whatever!' widens the divide.

Wrinkles

Wrinkles on the forehead are called Worry Lines.
I named mine Concern Crevices.
They developed from caring about people I love
during their trying times.
Between the brow they're Frown Lines.
Mine are Command Crumples.
Formed from disciplining children that I am responsible for,
without words, in hope they grow up to be respectful
of their surroundings, and of others.
Around the eyes they're Crow's Feet.
Those are my Comic Crinkles;
forged by hours and hours of laughter.
Around the lips they're referred to as Smoker's Lines.
I call mine Pucker Pleats.
Brought on by giving and receiving a lifetime's
worth of kisses.
Most will recognize the wrinkles and
attribute them to my age, but the reflection
I see staring back at me...
shows a lifetime of Love and Laughter.

Independence

An independent streak a mile wide
often leads one down deserted streets.

Soul Peace

As dawn breaks on a new day, the Sun
fights to be seen through the fog.
Yet, I am the victor as their war
brings peace to my soul.

Back To Back

Her mind keeps replaying his goodbye,
like a sad movie sound track.
The bartender knows the look of love gone wrong,
so he lines 'em up back to back.

His wedding band gleams red 'neath neon,
just another sign there's trouble.
The bartender recognizes the face of guilt too late,
so he pours the man a double.

From the table in the corner,
a young man races to the bar full throttle.
The bartender reading from the girl,
"He doesn't stand a chance"
while twisting the tops off two bottles.

Through all of his years behind a bar,
there's one truth he's come to believe.
No matter what, or how much you drink,
your problems go with you when you leave.

Perseverance

Perseverance is not proud, or boastful.
Like you, it is merely grace in constant motion.

Courage Roars

It's an uphill battle to get up this hill,
but I have done just that.
Because of this accomplishment
I offer these words to you...
When courage roars...mountains move.

Trust Your Gut

Never doubt your gut, for inside you
is an enchanted truth.
The wolf at your door may well
have been sent to guard your heart.

Three Wishes

When it's time to depart this Earth
I pray that I will have loved,
all the way from my toenails,
with no thought of consequences.
That I will have laughed out loud,
so outrageously, at every opportunity,
that it will have forced others to join me.
But, my greatest hope is that I,
by even the slightest measure,
have been able to forgive myself.

Exploration

In order to test your boundaries
you must first step outside them.

Believers

Once falling stars
hit the ground
they become flowers
in the gardens
of those who believe
that dreams do come true.

Shine

Prying eyes destroy lives.
Luckily, whether they be
blinded by arrogance, or ignorance,
I remain invisible.
It's not deception
that obscures my reflection.
Rather, it's my highest
vibration of light, and
I've no intention to dim my soul
for those who've no desire to shine.

Failure

There is something to learn from every emotion.
Therefore, if we refuse to feel, we fail.

It's Time

Today, I am choosing
to release the obsessions,
learn from the lessons,
and appreciate the blessings.

Perspective

The darkest of shadows
are the result of the
brightest of lights.
Which you focus on
depends on whether
your head is down, or
whether you choose
to look up.

Be A Beacon

The art of Paying It Forward
has been around for eons.
It serves as a beacon of hope
in a selfish world.
It comes directly from the
birth place of compassion,
is fostered by karma,
and is kept alive by selfless souls
on a mission to leave this world
a little better off than they found it.
Be a beacon.

Overcome

We must overcome
the crippling notion
that diversity breeds adversity.
In truth, diversity
breeds possibility.

Always Dream

Precious child, you've outgrown my arms, but are
no less loved than the day you were born. You ask
why I raised you as I did. I did what I thought
would serve you best.

Yes, I let you fall, I wanted you to learn to pick
yourself up, as often times there will be no one
around to help you.

Yes, I forced you to get yourself out of messes
that were of your own making. I wanted you
to learn that your actions have consequences
so that you might think before acting.

I may have appeared a little aloof at times,
but that couldn't be farther from the truth.
For every time you hurt - I hurt tenfold.
You asked how I survived some of the things
you'd done, and I can say with absolute
certainty that it was only by prayer. And now
you know why my knees are in such bad shape!

As I look back on the woman you've become
my chest swells with pride. Know, that to this
day I am still praying for you.

Dear Father,
Thank you for getting her to this point. Now,
I ask that you give her a heart overflowing with
love. A mind that stays focused, yet always
dreams. And, faith to know that without You -
neither she, nor I, would have survived her raising. Amen.

Perception

Memory alters the
recollection of pain
when the heart still loves.

Share Your Story

Survival stories become instruction manuals
for those in the midst of a storm.
Share your story!

A Kiss

You'll find enchantment in the kiss that is born
of possibility, not expectation.

Succeeding

I am shaped by every pair
of hands that have done
me wrong. My backbone
was strengthened each time
I fell to my knees.
Whenever I ran, face first,
into a wall it taught me
to keep my head up,
and my eyes focused forward.
Remarkably, I am succeeding
in spite of every mistake
I have ever made.

Dirty Knees

Before you go passing judgement
by what you think you see, you'd
be wise to remember that the sinner
and the saint both have dirty knees.

The Great Unknown

You've been there,
you've done that,
and you cannot stay.
Your past is the catalyst
guiding your way.
The seeds of the future
have all been sown.
It's all waiting for you
in the great unknown.

Juggling

Be careful child.
Trying to juggle
the weight of the
world may cause
you to spill
your dreams.

Searching

The heart searching for its beat
has no more concept of distance
than the soul searching for its
mate is able to comprehend time.

Dear Universe

Dear Universe,
I know that love comes
in your time, and when
you choose to send him.
Please know that I don't
have to be his whole world.
All I ask is that this time around,
I get to be the part
that love fucks
in the good way.

Say Something

Often, too many
words are used,
and not enough
is ever said.

Love Language

Love is the language the soul hears,
but the mind struggles to comprehend.
Therefore, the heart interprets.

Backbone

You're born with a spine,
but your backbone doesn't
form until you decide that
your tailbone has hit the
ground for the last time.

Afterlife

Few understand the possibility
of the first day past this life.
But I?
I have died too many times to
believe there is no life after this.

Aging

Fear not the reality of aging
for wrinkles are not visible
to those who see your soul.

The Dirt Road

Life is a highway, and I took the dirt road.
There have been some hellacious potholes,
along with a couple of detours I never expected.
But, I have seen some absolutely breathtaking scenery,
and had the pleasure to meet some amazing people.
No, I didn't take the highway, but it's been one hell of a ride,
and I can't wait to see where this road leads me.

The Heart's Shield

A shield of pure love's armor
is the only protection a heart
has from the insistences of its
two greatest foes...ego and self-doubt.

Master Gardener

You planted hope where only seeds of doubt
had ever grown.
With eternal gratitude I will nurture that hope
until it roots in my soul.

Possibilities

Buried 'neath the weight of
obligation and expectation
lies a soul eager to explore the
possibilities of imagination
and transformation.

Dear Child

Dear Child,
I have but two wishes for your life.
First, I wish that you Live to Learn.
Always let curiosity be the driving force of your soul,
and never stop asking questions.
My second, and most important wish,
is that you Learn to Live.
Learn to Live Child, for that is the key to happiness.

Never Give Up

I have no concern what your religion is, or isn't.
Does your heart know love?

Your gender is of no consequence to me.
Is your heart capable of love?

I have no thought for the color of your skin.
Though I would like to know, what color
is your heart?

Love wears many disguises, and often
makes the search seem impossible.
Yet, a pure heart will find another.
Be open in your search, more importantly,
never give up.

Blessings

Blessings are delivered to those
whose faith doesn't allow them
to expect anything less.

Be A Friend

You know that one friend you have,
the one who is there for everyone?
Ready whenever anyone needs them?
Everyone's rock?
Yeah, that one.
Give them a call...they may well be
needing someone, too.

Life's Lessons

A lapse in love's logic is a lesson,
not a life sentence.

Go Get It

We all have scarred hearts and bruised egos,
but life isn't a pissing contest.
So get up, get out, and get on with living.

Never Settle

Expect love to have gentle hands, a soft voice,
a tender heart, and a fierce passion.
Never settle for less.

Quilts

Old friends and new friends, lovers and kin,
No matter which state, or country you're in.
Whether we met through work, or through play,
It all boils down to this at the end of the day...

You've all become blocks in the quilt called My Life,
A comforter through toils, and everyday strife.
My security blanket when facing uncertain things,
Always at the ready for whatever life brings.

As I sit here nestled in thoughts of all you,
I want to say, "I love you" and "Thank You", too.
And, make sure you know I feel blessed to the hilt,
For this wonderful chance to be a block in Your Quilt.

CHAPTER 6

LITTLE MORE

Old Soul

I'm just an old soul with a deep inkwell.

LAUGHTER

Pilgrim's Parables
are the ramblings of a middle-aged woman
attempting to grow older with grace and a belly laugh.

#1 - My hair has gotten so long that if I stretch out the curl
it goes all the way down to where my boob used to be!

#2 - One of the good things about this age?
My chin hairs have turned gray making it harder for people
to see the ones I missed plucking!

#3 - If I had known my body would wear out so quickly
I would have bought an extended warranty!

#4 - I used to be finished with Christmas shopping by now,
yet here I sit eating the Halloween candy that I bought
not to hand out.

#5 - At this age when I buy alcohol and get carded,
I show 'em my boobs in appreciation.

#6 - You can't put a price on love, but
a divorce attorney sure can.

Oh, Well.

Apparently, "Whiskey,
Cigars & Tattooed men
on Harleys" wasn't the
answers the job interviewer
was looking for when he
asked what my weaknesses were.

One Hump Or Two?

You're about as inconspicuous
as a camel on a used car lot.
Chanting all your best pick up lines
with the cadence of an auctioneer.
But, here's the deal...
I'm not buying what you're trying to sell, and
I'm damn sure not interested in your hump.

Those Three Little Words

Three little words flash
across my phone screen.
A sense of calm fills my
core as a grin breaks
across my face.
What a thrill I get when
I read "Battery Fully Charged."

You Get What You Give

To Untrue Friends,
Unfaithful Lovers,
and Men that I once married,
I raise my glass
to toast the past,
and may no one find where they're buried.

Rusty

There once was a girl named Rusty,
An hourglass figure and quite busty.
All the men in town
Tried to bed her down,
'Til they found out her panties were crusty.

Nothing Compares

Nothing compares to that 70's style.
Hip huggers, hot pants, chokers and mood rings.
Mini skirts, and maxi dresses, meanwhile
TV's influence brought hair styles with wings,
Ponchos and gauchos, vests with fringe that swings.
Halter tops, pea coats, wrap skirts and jumpsuits.
And, no shoe today can top dingo boots.

The Jester

You come around with a stirring
beneath your loincloth.
Waving your scepter, and expecting me
to be grateful for the honor of your presence.
I finally figured out that you're the King of
assholes, and you're not worth the lost sleep,
or the dirty sheets.

Discombobulated

I get near you and either my thingamajig
gets all catawampus,
or my whatchamacallit
becomes discombobulated.
So, this is what love's like, huh?

If

If you intend to cheat...
You can't cheat Karma, she's a bitch.
If you intend to lie...
Lie in the middle of a busy street.
And, if you intend to leave...
Leave fresh batteries.

No More

She heard the whispers, and knew they'd never understand
that the smile on her face,
and the spring in her step
were all because she had no fucks left to give.

LIBERTY

Not Forgotten

Though now you're gone
Time soldiers on
In our war with the daily grind.

In these lives we've designed
We've become blind
To the sacrifices that got us here.

You confronted your fears
Despite the youth in your years
Facing enemies we can't imagine.

Not knowing all that happened
Yet, humbled by compassion
As we stand before their graves.

If just for today
Let us pause to say
Hero, you're gone but not forgotten.

The Homecoming

Like generations before,
Chest swelling pride is displayed.
Volunteering for service as history is made.

Fighting in the trenches,
Lonely, tired, and afraid.
Masking the fear with a bravado charade. (Continued)

Boys become warriors,
As strong men are made.
For a Soldier's place very few would take trade.

They've no want for a marching band,
Nor ticker tape parade.
A homecoming with loved ones is for what they've prayed.

If that's not what will be granted,
Then Father I ask they be repaid,
With a seat beside You for the life that they gave.

Battered And Bloody Souls

Having spent their share of time in Hell,
To Earth's demons they bid farewell.
From their service they're granted release,
They'll spend eternity in blissful peace.
Tattered clothes, and muddy boots,
Yet to each one, Jesus salutes.
For all war's battered and bloody souls,
Are forever welcomed into Heaven's fold.

Our Hero

You signed on a line,
to protect me and mine,
without even knowing our name.

You'd give up your life,
without thinking twice,
to keep lit Liberty's flame.
(Continued)

Your pride you maintain,
when our flag's on display,
to do over, you'd do just the same.

With resounding drums,
when St. Peter comes,
And the Angels call out your name.

You've defended with courage,
so our Country could flourish,
To the Heavens, our Hero,
may your soul take aim.

Freedom Rings

We stand, we sit,
We seem to forget,
We are One Nation.

They pledge, they fight,
They wonder why,
For an ungrateful nation.

I'll honor, I'll pray,
For their safety each day,
On behalf of a grateful nation.

I'll stand, I'll sing,
May freedom forever ring,
In this wonderful, glorious, nation.

LETTERS

Rhyme

I oft' use rhyme,
as I step back in time,
to tell you who I am.
I seldom know,
where the words will go,
or how they'll explain where I've been.
Wishing you decipher,
how I conspire,
to show that I am real.
Yet I can't find the words,
not one noun or verb,
to tell you how I feel.

Tourniquet

The words spill out
across the paper like blood
from a tapped vein.
Yet, a tourniquet would only
increase the pain.
So, I'll write for eternity
drop by drop.
All the while knowing
the flow from lost love
there's no way to stop.

All Knowing

The mighty pen describes a kiss only the writer has tasted.

Rewrite

Another sleepless night,
Another early morning.
I sit here with only the company of memories.

With this ink I will rewrite our story.
I will write in that you always loved me.
And, that you chose me.
And, that I died in your arms when we were old and gray.

Reciprocated Love

A shattered heart led me to splatter ink.
Eventually I traded my loss of you
in on a love of words.
On those days when I am able to
not write of you, the words love me back.

Tears And Blood

I have no rules for this pen.
It tends to wander where I've already been.
Across years, and miles, and hearts it travels.
Oft' forcing ties that bind to unravel.
Creating harmonious contradictions,
or spurring along emotional transitions.
When pressed to paper the words do flood.
Formed from the ink of my tears, and blood.

Scribbling

I scribble sentences
without hesitation.
Yet, as our story unfolds
I have reservations.

What color ink?
And, how many pages?
Am I writing of days?
Or, a love for the ages?

There'll be pages of lust
in the Story of Us.
With plenty of laughter
penned in each chapter.

And, if our love dies
before the story should end,
My pen and I...
the truth we shall bend.

The End

Time flies
once the ink is dry
on the page
where we swore "I Do".

Now the ink is wet
as we pen our regret
on the page
where we swear "I'm Through".

Mute Heart

She writes of lust and love,
and all the things her heart speaks of.
He tells her that her words are beautiful.
What he doesn't know is that before him,
her heart was mute.

Spilled Ink

Memories spill from the tip of my pen.
Letters form words to validate our years.
Each splashing around in pools of dropped tears.
Drowning recollections as the ink smears.
Hopeful to never write of pain again.

Secrets

Never tell your secrets to the pen.
They'll always end up on paper.

Just A Trace

I trace these words
from inside my soul.
Hiding between lines
of stories left untold.
Hoping someone cares
enough to read,
the tales I write
with the ink I bleed.

Definition

I find you scribbled
inside every word
my heart uses
to define love.

Executioner

The parchment and ink are my saviors.
Wrong me, and they will be
your executioner.

The Spell

The most mysterious element of the written word
is its ability to conjure a different illusion
for each soul who partakes of its incantations.

Found

I smile while tracing my finger along
your writing; imagining the love
in your hand as you penned my name.
Drawing the envelope to my nose,
inhaling the fading fragrance
of your cologne. The soft aroma
has me longing to hold you in my arms.
With a tear in my eye, and a tightness
in my chest, I reread the message inside.
Such a tender reminder that you are
indeed the man that I prayed would find me.

Beautiful Words

You say that you admire the beauty in the words I pen.
While you don't speak in rhyme, or metered verse,
every word that crosses your lips is adorned with sincerity.
That is every bit as beautiful as anything I am able to write.

Exorcism

I write with a simple plan in mind;
use words to exorcise the demons
that haunt the walls of my heart,
and the halls of my soul.

Last Words

My last words I will not take to my grave.
As my poor, tired, heart pumps its last few drops of blood
they will spill as ink onto the page.
Immortalizing for eternity that I died loving you.

To My Grave

There's a letter in the drawer beside my bed.
When I'm gone I don't want it read.
It's filled with things I wish I'd said;
Love's bidding I should have pled.
But, pride kept the words unsaid.
So to my gave they'll go instead.

Love, Your Child

Dear Mom and Dad,

I know you're nervous, and you want
to shelter me from all you went through,
but I have lessons to learn. I have a few
pointers to make life easier on all of us.

Don't tell me "No" then change your mind
when I throw a fit. Instead, teach me the
power of conviction and that No means No.

Don't let me be disrespectful of you, or
others. Teach me that respect is only
given when it's earned.

Don't shield me from troubles, tragedy,
or even death. Teach me perseverance,
and of the finality of death, so that I may
better appreciate life, and those I love.

There's more, and most I will forget
before I get there. I'm sure we'll learn
more as we grow. I know you think you
had it hard and want life to be different
for me, but as I see it, you didn't turn out
so bad.

I love you both, and I'll meet you soon!

Love,
Your Child

LOYALTY

Not Going Anywhere

I hear the tiredness in your voice,
and I know just how very thin you are stretched.
I'm of little help other than words of encouragement,
and prayers.
Please know that those will never cease,
and I'm not going anywhere.

Courage

By watching you I have learned that no
matter how low I get, I can go on.

I know with all certainty this to be true
because I witness you doing it every day.

Your heart bares unfathomable burdens,
yet you rise, and keep moving forward.

Your tenacity is the most awe inspiring
display of courage that I have ever had
the honor of witnessing.

I owe a debt of gratitude that I have
no way to repay, other than to lead
by your example.

Shine

I stare in awe at the light shining
through the cracks in your soul.
Most won't recognize the beauty
in having walked through the fires
of hell as being the source.
Some have forgotten that survival
is so damn beautiful.
Shine!
Let your light blind them all to
remind them of strength's beauty.

Deja Vu

Deja Vu is a whisper
from the Universe
to your soul.
A gentle reminder
that at this moment in time,
you are exactly where you should be.

Deep Waters

When I finally open the floodgates,
and my story starts pouring out,
it will be because I trust you to be a
strong enough swimmer to save us both.

God's Own Grace

I whispered a prayer for you,
I know the hell you're going through.

Choked by death's expertise,
Sorrow knocks you to your knees.

Letting no one witness fragility,
While cursing limited capability.

Believing you fight this battle alone,
Fearing your strength will be overthrown.

In the inevitable bereavement that you face,
Don't forget you're protected by God's Own Grace.

Determined

He's a wolf of a different breed.
His heart leads him to places he can't see.
His determination is unwavering.
He scaled the wall with bravery,
As his fearless heart led him to me.

The Same Road

There is such comfort in finding someone
who has walked the same road as you.
Especially, when you have walked the hard road.

You Are

Your arms provide a cornerstone
of strength; your heart is an abyss
of endless love.
You are the epitome of everything
that I have searched for.
I needed a rock when I stumbled
upon the mountain of a man
that you are.

Impossible

Falling in love with you was hard.
My head put up one hell of a fight,
but my heart won.
The only thing that they agree on is,
that now, falling out of love with you
would be impossible.

Daily Prayer

Since you've gone I've managed to break away
from most of the routines that centered around you.
However, there is one habit that I refuse to release.

Until my last breath I will whisper a prayer for you,
every day.

An imploration that you find the peace, love, and
happiness that has eluded you in this lifetime.

I sincerely hope you have found a piece, or two, within these covers that touched you. For me, the 300+ pieces contained herein were easier to write than this About The Author page. Often this page is written by someone who knows the Author well, or by someone who has been told the Author's story. I choose to tell you my story as I am the one who knows it well.

I was lucky enough to be born and raised in the four states area of the great state of Texas. I like to say that it was just enough Texas to get the accent and the pride. Anyone who has lived in Texas can appreciate that statement as the gospel. Anyone who hasn't, will consider it as the bragging that Texans are known for. Both of those statements are true.

I married my Senior year in High School. As soon as I graduated, we hit the road with work. During that marriage I was graced with the most amazing soul for a daughter. Nineteen years later we chose to undo the I Do. Three years later I did the I Do again.

After that marriage was undone I decided to move back to Texas as that's where my immediate family lives. So thirty years, nineteen states, and two ex-husbands later, here I am again.

I'd like to have one of those stories about having written my whole life, but that's not mine. Not long after moving back, I reconnected with a friend from High School. Three years later that ended in a miserable break-up. Believe me when I say that a heartbreak hurts just as badly when you're middle aged as it does at 16. That heartbreak resulted in my putting pen to paper for the first time.

Along with writing, I enjoy a bourbon, and a fine cigar. I cuss. I pray. I laugh out loud. Mostly, I just hope that I leave this life having made someone else's slightly better.

I'm walking a path of writing that I never dreamed I would end up on. I stumble, and I question each turn, but I continue to pour out parts of myself to those interested in reading. I am blessed to have had the opportunity to connect with some priceless souls through social media. I appreciate those who interact with me daily as I believe that words are the conduits that connect our souls.

Much love,
Lisa Pilgrim
Connect with me on Facebook at Priceless Words by Lisa Pilgrim.

CPSIA information can be obtained
at www.ICGtesting.com
Printed in the USA
FSHW020629190321
79597FS

9 780578 811444